TRANSPORTATION!

BY GAIL GIBBONS

HOW PEOPLE GET AROUND

Holiday House / New York

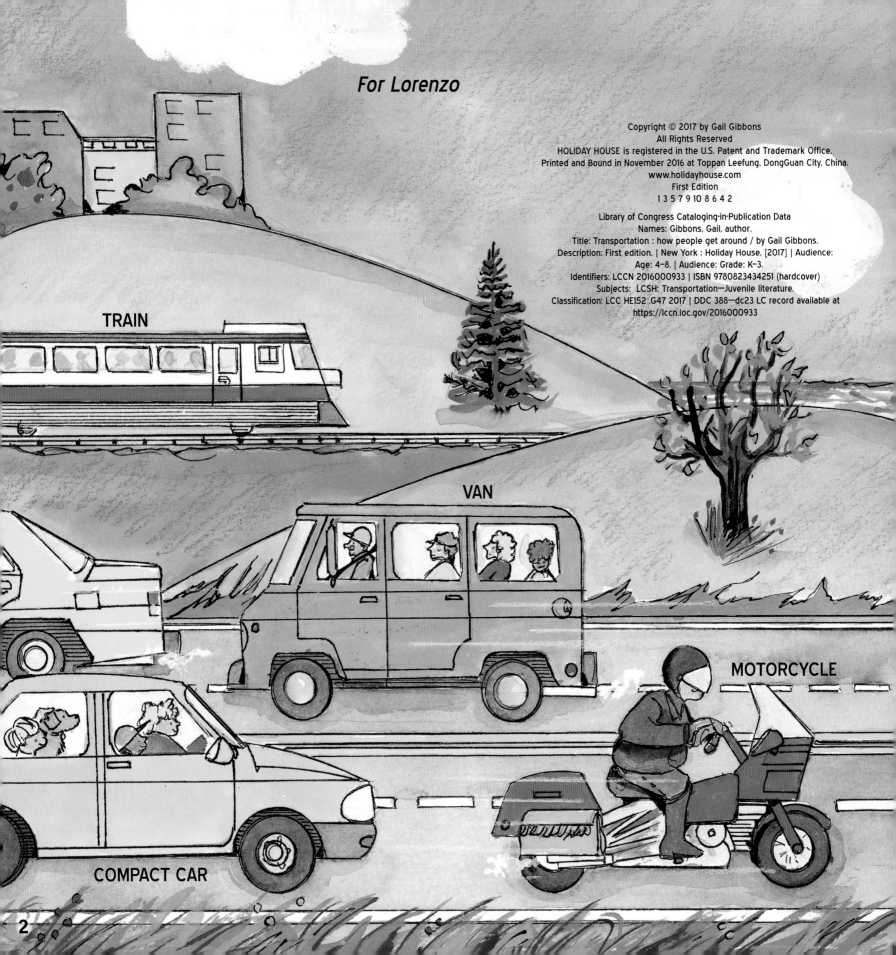

For Lorenzo

Library of Congress Cataloging-in-Publication Data
Names: Gibbons, Gail, author.
Title: Transportation : how people get around / by Gail Gibbons.
Description: First edition. | New York : Holiday House, [2017] | Audience:
Age: 4–8. | Audience: Grade: K–3.
Identifiers: LCCN 2016000933 | ISBN 9780823434251 (hardcover)
Subjects: LCSH: Transportation—Juvenile literature.
Classification: LCC HE152 .G47 2017 | DDC 388—dc23 LC record available at
https://lccn.loc.gov/2016000933

TRAIN

VAN

MOTORCYCLE

COMPACT CAR

Transportation is what people use to get around. They choose what works best to get from place to place.

CARS AND OTHER VEHICLES

SCOOTER

CARS also called
AUTOMOBILES

TWO-DOOR
PICKUP TRUCK

MINIVAN

Drivers and passengers travel on roads . . .

4

CITY TRANSIT BUS

LANE

SHUTTLE BUS

STATION WAGON

COMPACT CAR

. . . and highways.

5

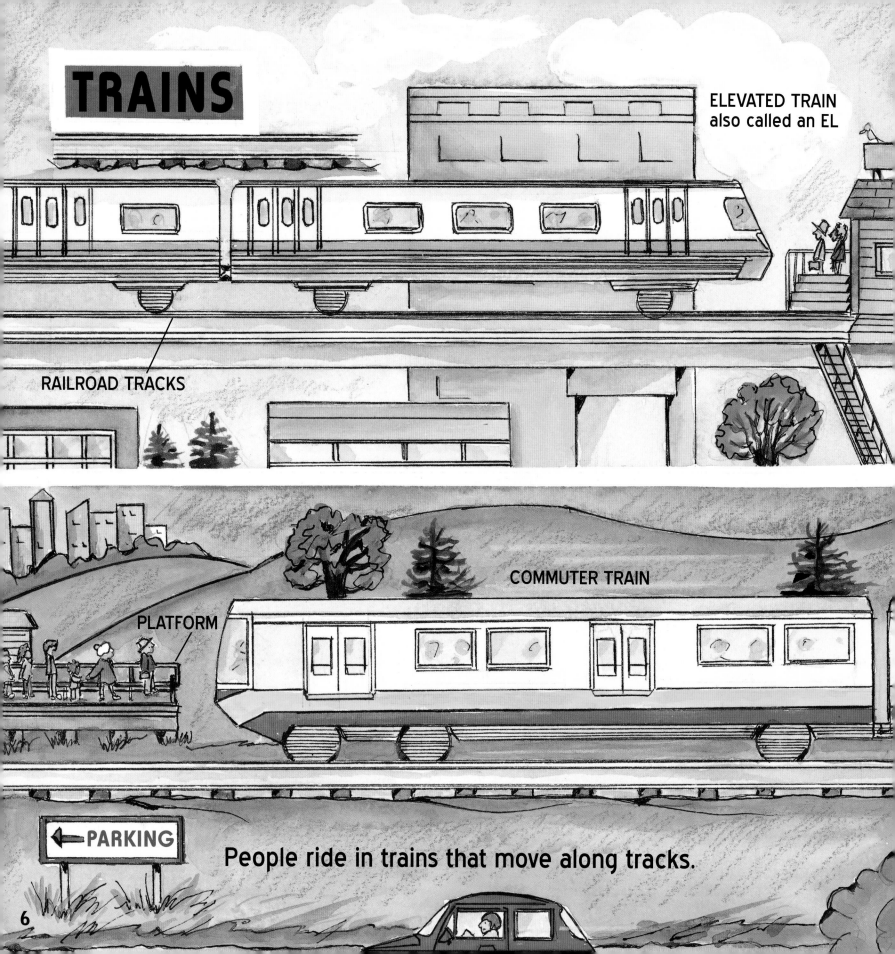

TRAINS

ELEVATED TRAIN
also called an EL

RAILROAD TRACKS

COMMUTER TRAIN

PLATFORM

← PARKING

People ride in trains that move along tracks.

AIRCRAFT

SMALL
PROPELLER
PLANE

PROPELLERS

LARGE
JET
PLANE

JET ENGINE

Some people fly through the sky in airplanes.

BOATS

SMALL POWERBOAT
or MOTORBOAT

Very large BOATS are called SHIPS.

CRUISE SHIP

People use boats to move across the water.

Some people shop nearby.

HATCHBACK

People need to get to work.

SUBWAY TRAIN

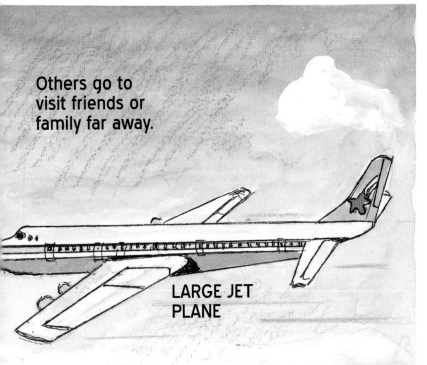

Others go to visit friends or family far away.

LARGE JET PLANE

Some people use boats for fun.

SAILBOAT

Some people travel short distances, while others go to faraway places.

CARS AND OTHER VEHICLES

CONVERTIBLE CAR

SUV means SPORTS UTILITY VEHICLE.

LARGE SUV

MINICAR

FOUR-DOOR PICKUP TRUCK

There are many different sizes and shapes of cars and other vehicles that travel on roadways.

BICYCLES

JEEP

SMALL SUV

COUPE

SPORTS CAR

There are many ways for people to get around.

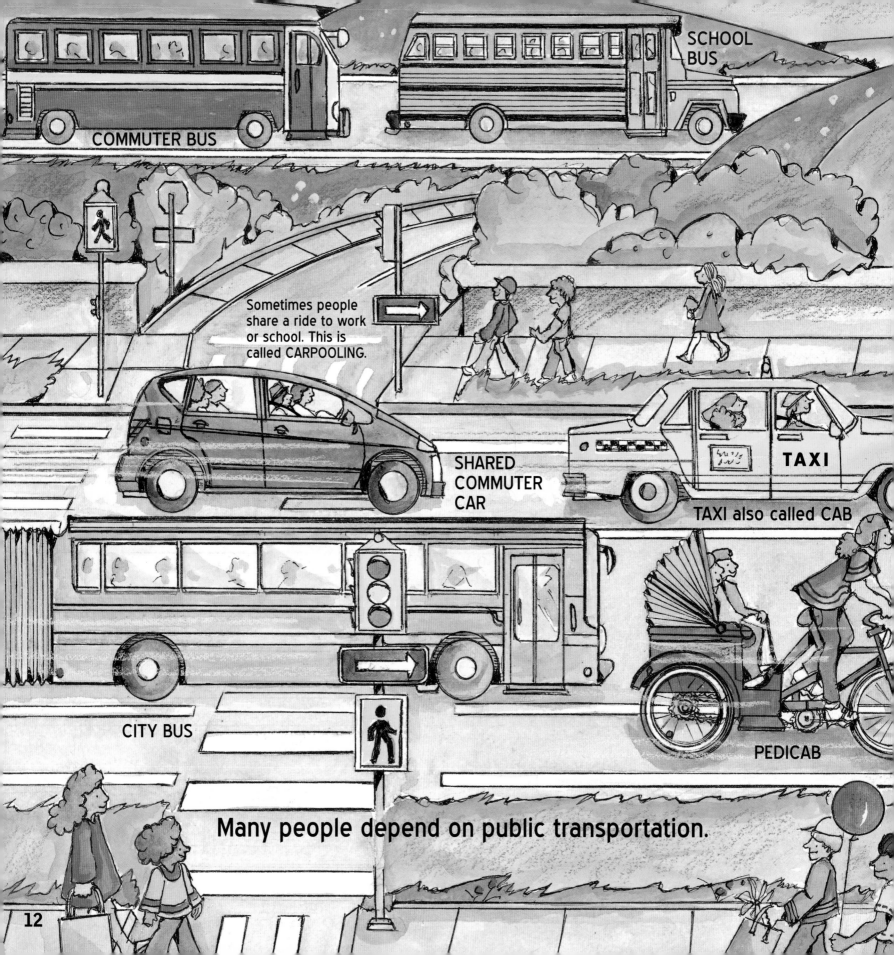

COMMUTER BUS

SCHOOL BUS

Sometimes people share a ride to work or school. This is called CARPOOLING.

SHARED COMMUTER CAR

TAXI

TAXI also called CAB

CITY BUS

PEDICAB

Many people depend on public transportation.

MINIBUS

DOUBLE-
DECKER
BUS

BICYCLE
MESSENGER

Every day many people travel to and from the same places,
such as work or school. They are called commuters.

SPEED LIMIT 55

LUXURY MOTOR COACH
also called a LUXURY COACH

LUXURY SEDAN

STRETCH LIMOUSINE

Often people want to travel in comfort. Some ride in luxury vehicles.

14

LARGE LUXURY RV

OFFICE

RV means RECREATIONAL VEHICLE.

CAMPER RV

RV TRAILER

CAMPGROUND

Some people own vehicles that have all the comforts of home.

15

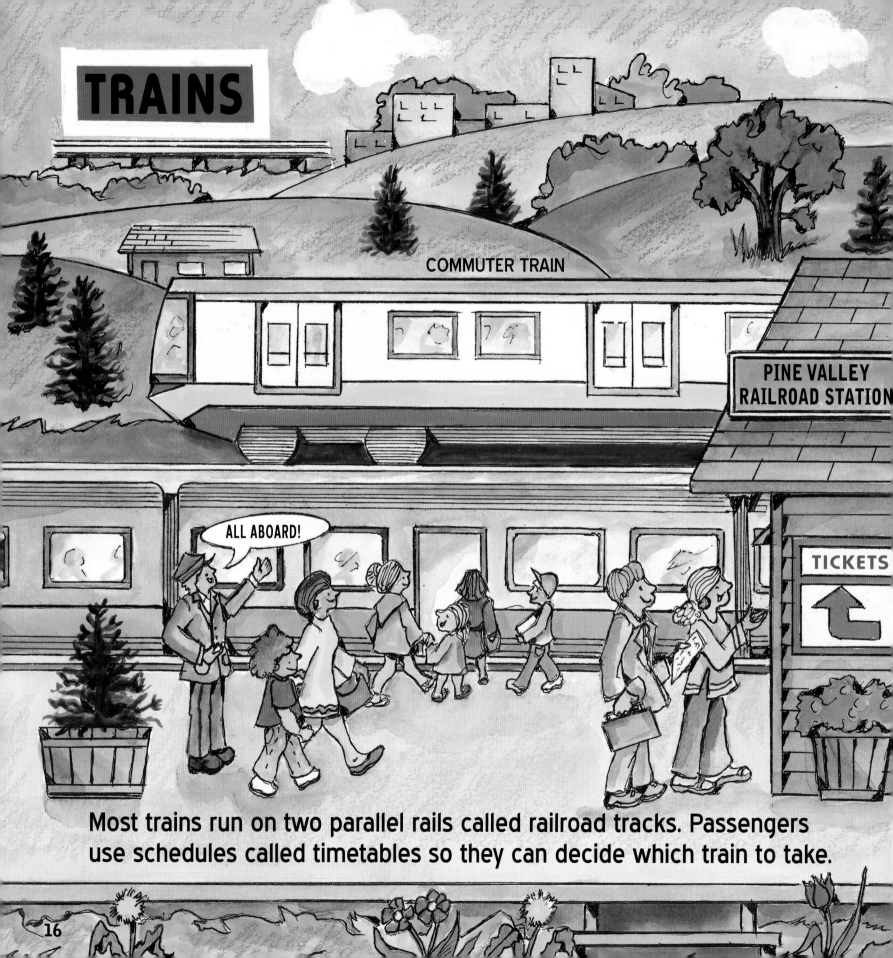

TRAINS

COMMUTER TRAIN

PINE VALLEY
RAILROAD STATION

ALL ABOARD!

TICKETS

Most trains run on two parallel rails called railroad tracks. Passengers use schedules called timetables so they can decide which train to take.

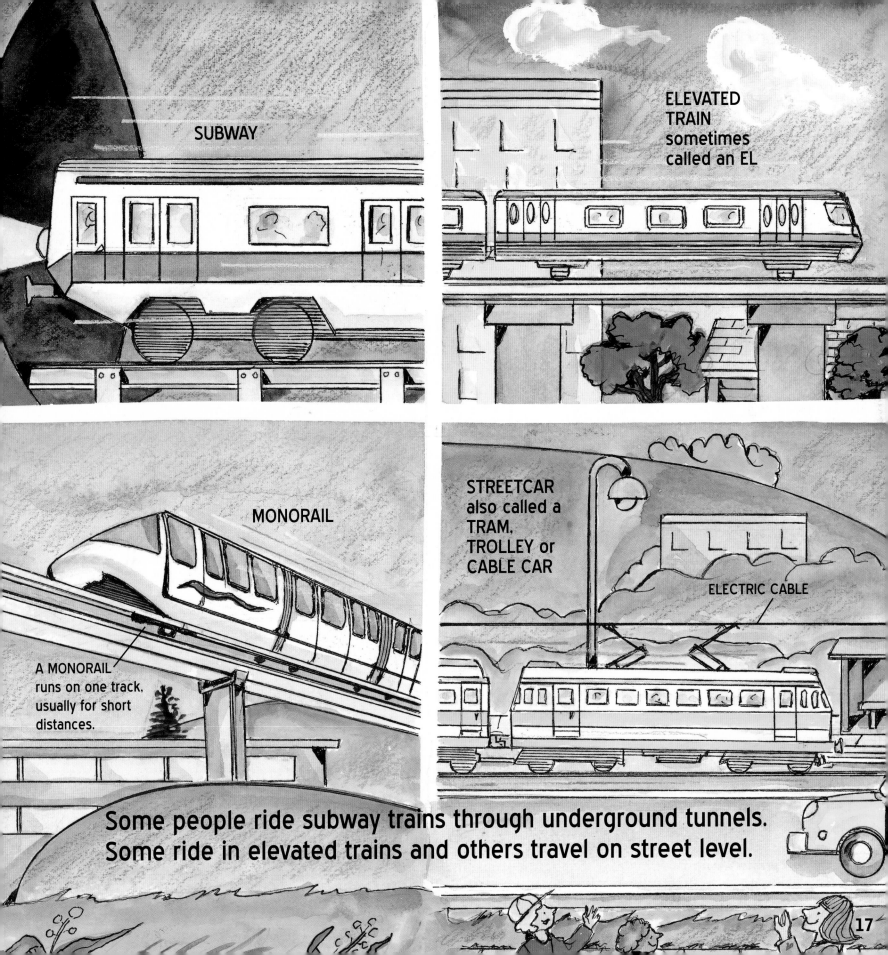

SUBWAY

ELEVATED TRAIN
sometimes called an EL

MONORAIL

A MONORAIL runs on one track, usually for short distances.

STREETCAR also called a TRAM, TROLLEY or CABLE CAR

ELECTRIC CABLE

Some people ride subway trains through underground tunnels.
Some ride in elevated trains and others travel on street level.

LONG-DISTANCE
PASSENGER TRAIN

Many passenger trains travel to faraway towns and cities.
Sometimes they have sleeping cabins and dining cars.

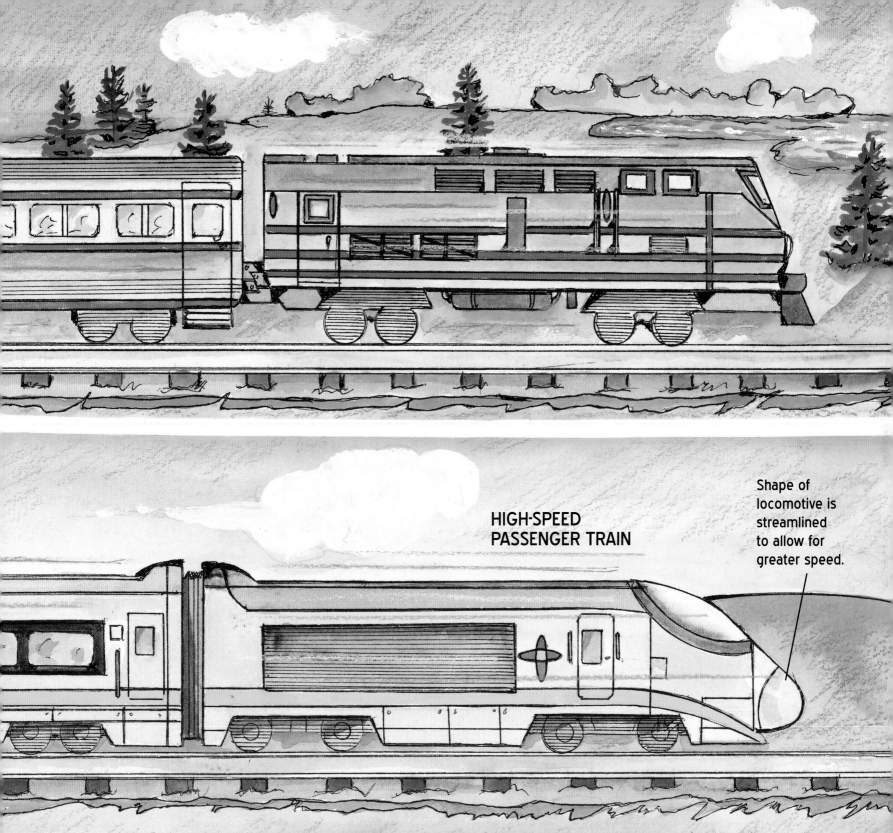

HIGH-SPEED
PASSENGER TRAIN

Shape of
locomotive is
streamlined
to allow for
greater speed.

High-speed trains move extremely fast. Passengers arrive at
their destinations very quickly.

AIRCRAFT

SMALL
PASSENGER
PLANE

PROPELLER
BLADES

HELICOPTER

PROPELLER
BLADES

A HELICOPTER
can move up and down,
forward and sideways.

A FLOAT PLANE
can land and take
off from water.

FLOAT PLANE

PONTOONS
or FLOATS

In the sky, there are small and large aircraft. Helicopters
and many planes have engines that turn propeller blades
to make them fly.

20

LARGE
PROPELLER
PLANE

There are large propeller planes that carry many passengers.

JET ENGINE

COMMUTER
JET PLANE

CORPORATE
JET PLANE

The CONTROL TOWER is where air traffic controllers communicate with pilots.

RUNWAY

SKYWAY

Jet planes come in many sizes and have powerful jet engines.

LARGE
COMMERCIAL
JET

Some jet planes are huge. They can fly many passengers to faraway places.

BOATS

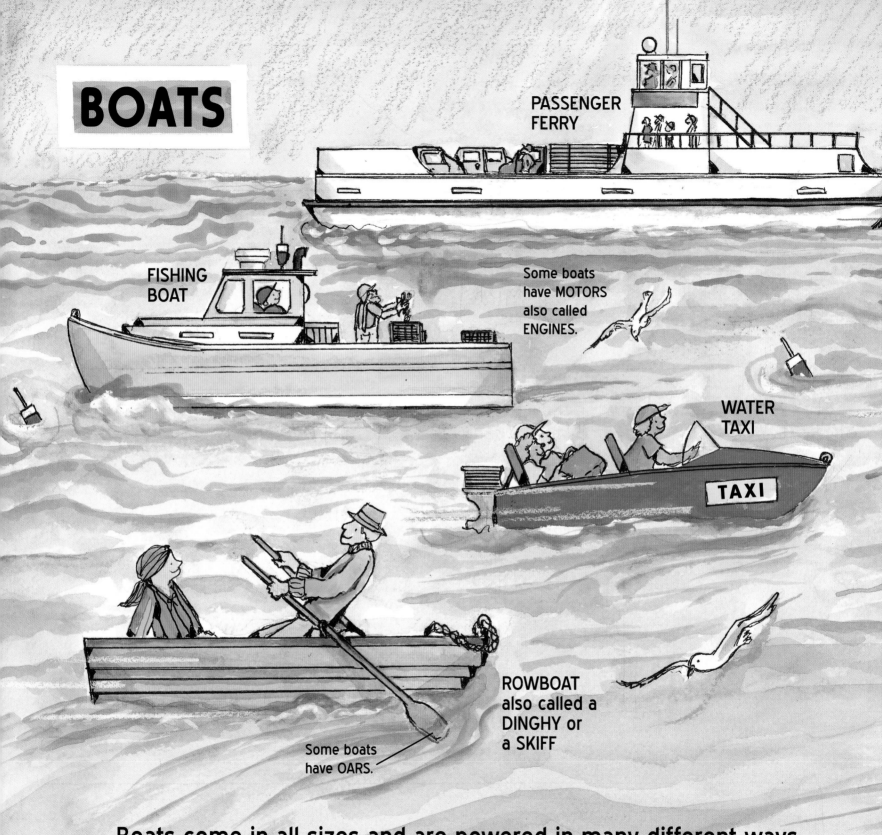

PASSENGER FERRY

FISHING BOAT

Some boats have MOTORS also called ENGINES.

WATER TAXI

TAXI

ROWBOAT also called a DINGHY or a SKIFF

Some boats have OARS.

Boats come in all sizes and are powered in many different ways. Some are workboats.

Some boats have SAILS that catch the wind.

YACHT

SAILBOAT

PADDLE

KAYAK

Some boats have PADDLES.

CANOE

PADDLE

Some are pleasure boats.

YAWL

SIGHTSEEING
BOAT

Some larger boats carry lots of passengers.

CRUISE SHIP
also called
CRUISE LINER

Cruise ships carry many passengers on trips to see many sights.

TRANSPORTATION IN SPACE

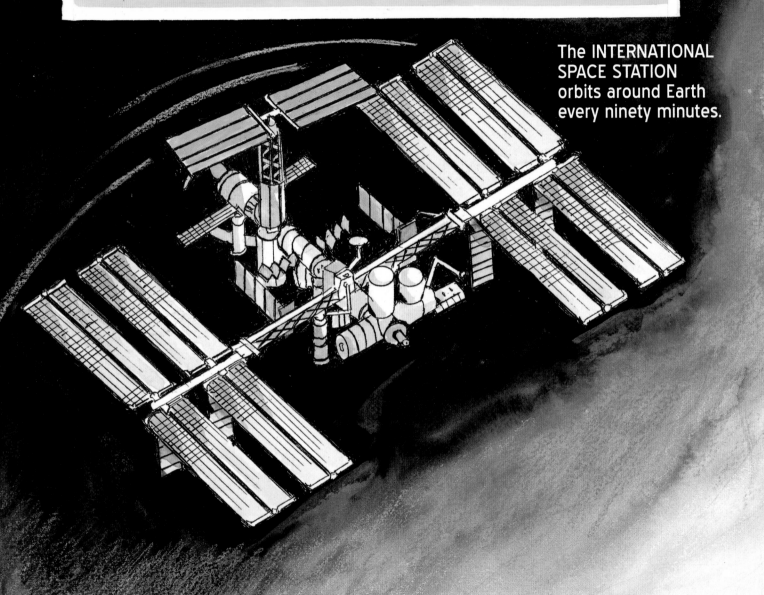

The INTERNATIONAL SPACE STATION orbits around Earth every ninety minutes.

Astronauts, scientists and other trained people from all over the world travel to the International Space Station. They study space travel and do scientific experiments. In the future, people may travel in many new ways.

There are many ways for people to get around.

People are always on the go!

There is transportation everywhere!

IMPORTANT SIGNS, SIGNALS AND NAVIGATIONAL AIDS

SCHOOL ZONE

CARS AND OTHER VEHICLES

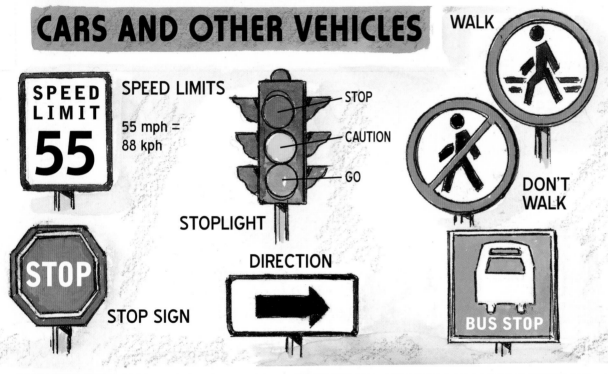

SPEED LIMITS

55 mph = 88 kph

SPEED LIMIT 55

STOPLIGHT
STOP
CAUTION
GO

STOP SIGN

DIRECTION

WALK

DON'T WALK

BUS STOP

RAILROAD CROSSING

RAIL ROAD CROSSING

GPS

TURN LEFT...

(GLOBAL SATELLITE POSITION)

TRAINS

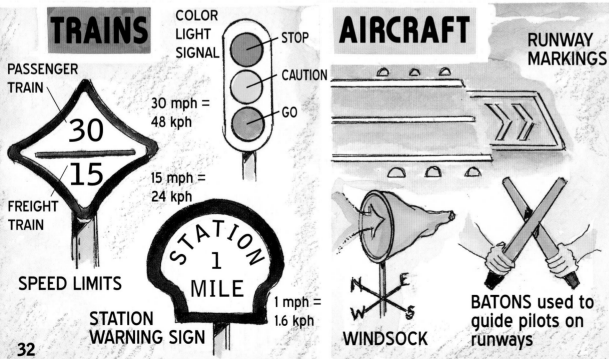

PASSENGER TRAIN

30
15

FREIGHT TRAIN

SPEED LIMITS

COLOR LIGHT SIGNAL
STOP
CAUTION
GO

30 mph = 48 kph

15 mph = 24 kph

STATION 1 MILE

1 mph = 1.6 kph

STATION WARNING SIGN

AIRCRAFT

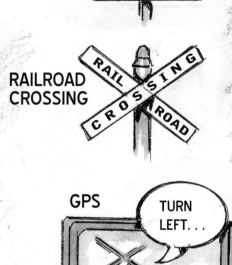

RUNWAY MARKINGS

WINDSOCK

BATONS used to guide pilots on runways

BOATS

BELL BUOY

LIGHTHOUSE

NAVIGATIONAL CHARTS